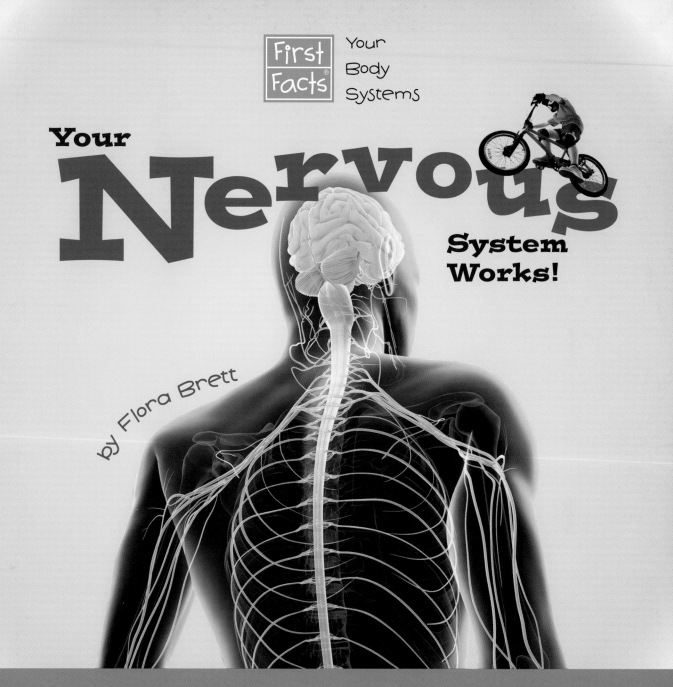

First Facts

Your Body Systems

Your Nervous System Works!

by Flora Brett

CAPSTONE PRESS

a capstone imprint

First Facts are published by Capstone Press,
1710 Roe Crest Drive, North Mankato, Minnesota 56003
www.capstonepub.com

Library of Congress Cataloging-in-Publication Data
Brett, Flora, author.
Your nervous system works! / by Flora Brett.
        pages cm. — (First facts. Your body systems)
Summary: "Engaging text and informative images help readers learn about their nervous system."— Provided by publisher.
Audience: Ages 6–9.
Audience: K to grade 3.
Includes bibliographical references and index.
ISBN 978-1-4914-2066-9 (library binding) — ISBN 978-1-4914-2250-2 (pbk.) —
ISBN 978-1-4914-2272-4 (ebook PDF)
1. Nervous system—Juvenile literature. 2. Brain—Juvenile literature. 3. Human physiology—Juvenile literature. I. Title.
QP361.5.B74 2015
612.8—dc23
                            2014023832

Editorial Credits
Emily Raij and Nikki Bruno Clapper, editors; Cynthia Akiyoshi, designer;
Svetlana Zhurkin, media researcher; Laura Manthe, production specialist

Photo Credits
Capstone, 7 (left); Capstone Studio: Karon Dubke, 5; Shutterstock: AntiMartina (dotted background), cover and throughout, BioMedical, 15, BlueRingMedia, 11, Denys Prykhodov, 4, Designua, 17 (top right), Fotoluminate LLC, 9, Mik Lav, 20, Sebastian Kaulitzki, cover, 1, 13, Steven Frame, 19, StudioSmart, 7 (top right), swissmacky, 21, Tomasz Trojanowski, cover (top right), back cover, 1 (top right), Viacheslav Nikolaenko, 17

Printed in the United States of America in North Mankato, Minnesota.
092014   008482CGS15

Table of Contents

How You Feel

Ouch!

You quickly move your hand away from the hot water. What made you do that? Your nervous system! Your nervous system is your body's message center. It tells your other body systems what to do and helps you think.

Your nerves, spinal cord, and brain make up your nervous system. Nerves are thin fibers. They send signals to your brain to control your actions and reactions.

nerve—a thin fiber that carries messages between the brain and other parts of the body

Nerves

Nerves look like bundles of gray threads. Your body has more nerves than you can count.

Nerves are made of cells called neurons. Most neurons have a cell body, an **axon**, and many **dendrites**. Inside the cell body is a **nucleus**, or control center. Dendrites look like short trees. They receive electric signals from other neurons. Long axons send these signals to other neurons. Signals move from neuron to neuron until they reach the brain.

axon—the part of a nerve cell that sends out signals

dendrite—a branch on a nerve cell that receives signals

nucleus—the command center of the cell that gives instructions to the other parts of the cell

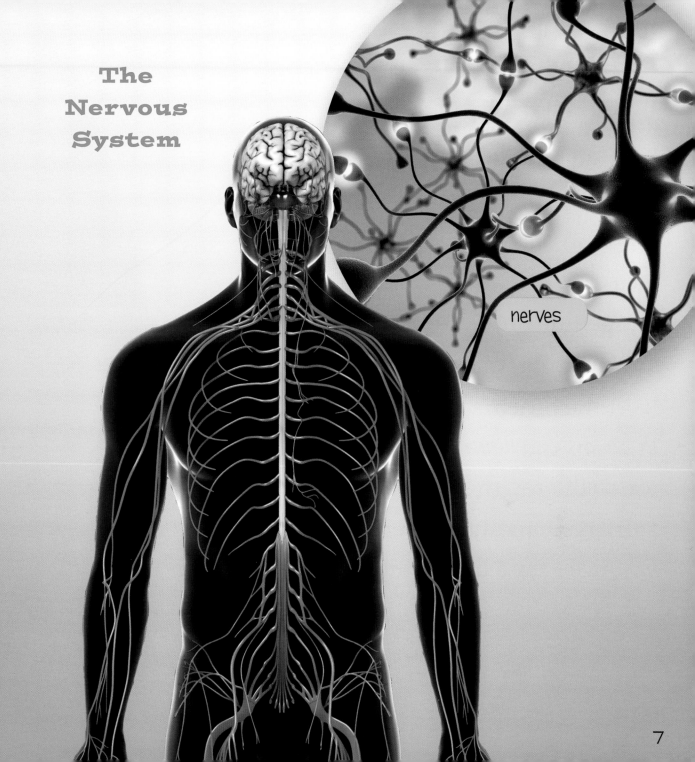

The Nervous System

nerves

Nerves and the Senses

Nerves gather information through sensors from your five senses. Sensors send messages through neurons. The messages tell your brain what is happening around you. Everything you sense turns into electrical signals.

At the beach, you use all five senses at once. You see the blue ocean and touch the rough sand. You smell sunscreen and hear waves. Finally, you taste the salty water.

9

Brain Basics

Electric signals travel to and from your brain through nerve pathways. As you learn facts and gain memories, your neurons form new pathways. These connections help you do things better and more easily.

Different parts of the brain have different jobs. The cerebrum controls learning, imagining, and memory. The brain stem connects the brain to the spinal cord. It controls involuntary muscles, such as the heart and breathing muscles. The cerebellum controls balance and body movement.

Fact:
Your brain makes enough electricity to power a lightbulb.

The Human Brain

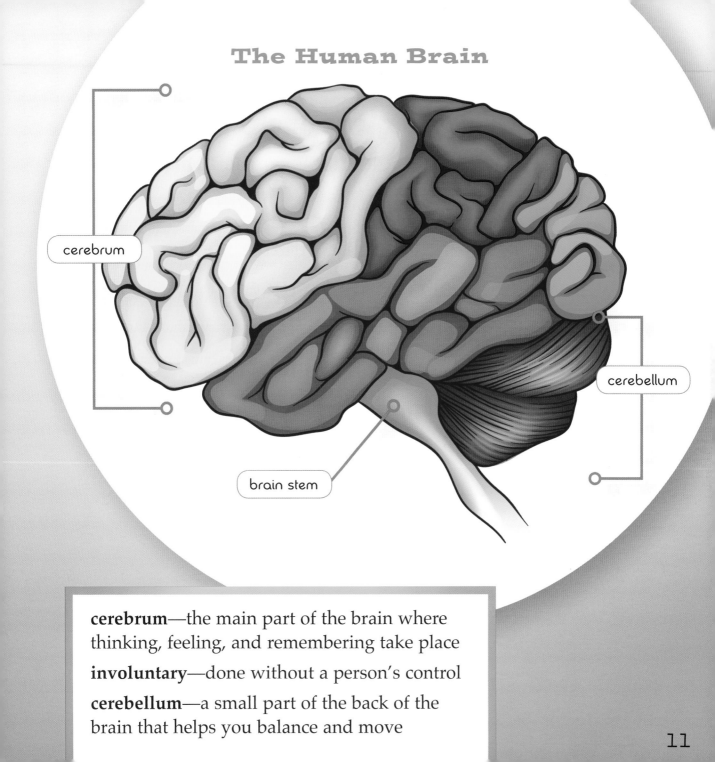

cerebrum

cerebellum

brain stem

cerebrum—the main part of the brain where thinking, feeling, and remembering take place

involuntary—done without a person's control

cerebellum—a small part of the back of the brain that helps you balance and move

11

Message System

Nerves branch out to every part of your body. Messages travel as electric signals along these pathways.

The nervous system is really three systems. Your brain and spinal cord make up the central nervous system. Nerves connect to the brain and spinal cord in the peripheral nervous system. The brain's hypothalamus helps control body temperature and the autonomic nervous system. This system controls things that happen automatically, such as breathing and digestion.

hypothalamus—your brain's temperature control

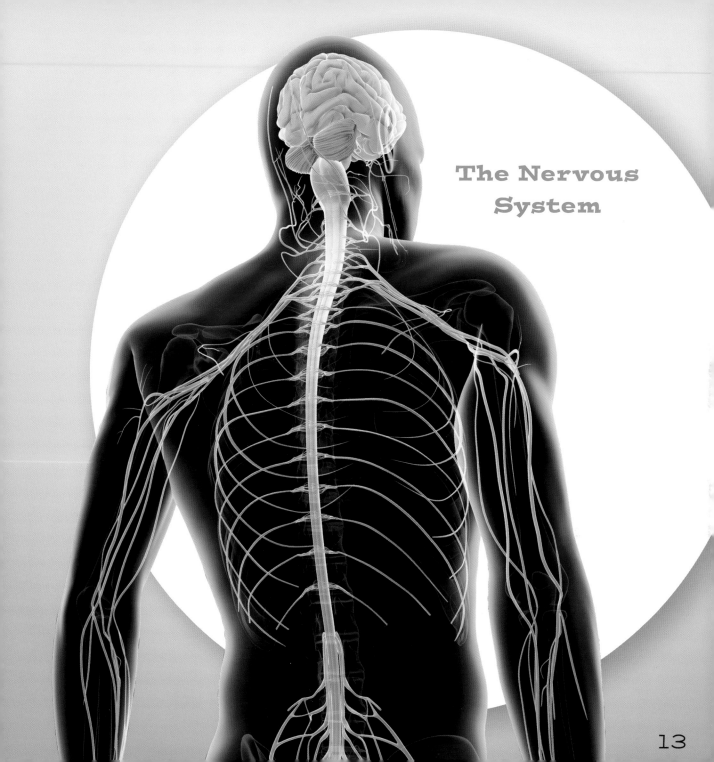

The Nervous System

Central Nervous System

The central nervous system controls the whole nervous system. Your brain is the control center. It receives information from your senses. Then it sends signals through your nerves. The signals tell your body what to do.

Inside your spine is your spinal cord. Your spinal cord is the main highway for nerve signals. These messages quickly move to and from the brain.

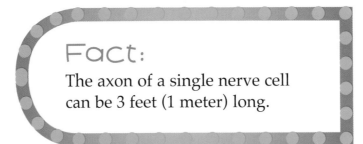

Fact:
The axon of a single nerve cell can be 3 feet (1 meter) long.

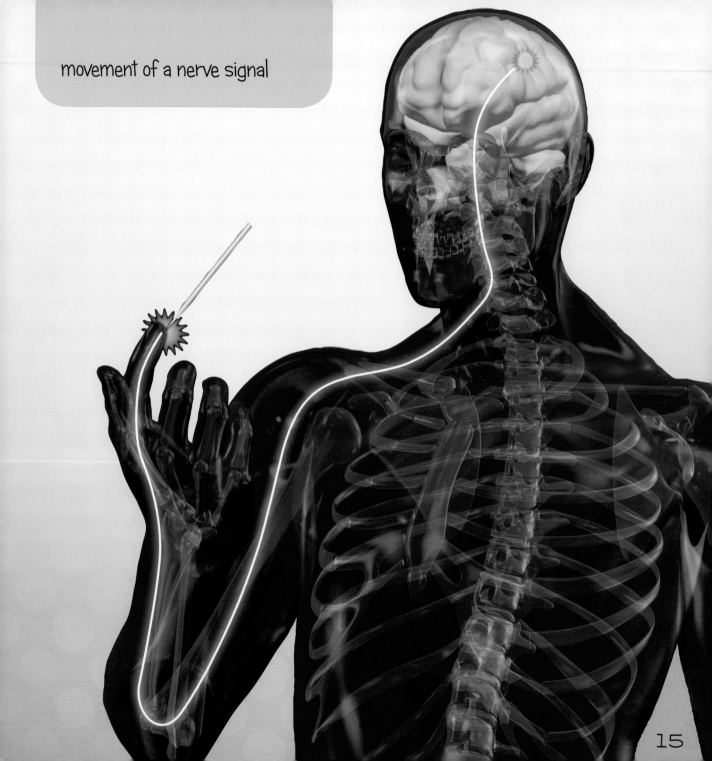

movement of a nerve signal

15

Nerves and Muscles

Your nervous system and muscular system work together to move your body. First, you think about moving. Then your brain sends signals to your muscles through your nerves. The signals make your muscles move.

Your involuntary muscles work automatically. Nerves signal the heart to pump blood. They tell your stomach muscles to digest food.

Fact:

Reflexes are automatic responses to threats to your body. When you touch a hot stove, nerves in your fingertips send an emergency signal to your brain telling you to move your hand.

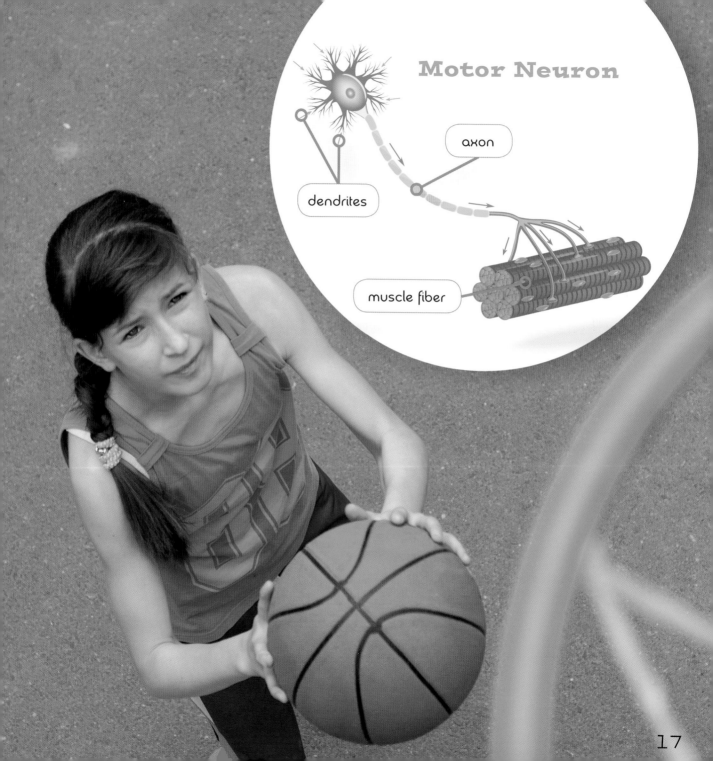

Motor Neuron

axon

dendrites

muscle fiber

17

Diseases and Drugs

Some diseases harm nerves. Parkinson's disease kills nerves that control muscles. Alzheimer's disease attacks nerves in the brain, causing memory loss.

Alcohol and drug use also harms nerves. Drugs can destroy nerves or change the way nerves work. Nerves are damaged every time a drug is taken. These nerves may never work correctly again.

Fact:

Nerve-cell damage from alcohol can cause neuropathy. People with neuropathy feel pain, burning, and weakness in their hands and feet.

Some people with a nerve disease must use a wheelchair.

Keeping Healthy

How can you keep your nervous system healthy? First, eat good foods. Fruits, vegetables, and other foods with minerals give you energy. Puzzles, music, and art keep your brain working and learning. Sleep lets your nervous system rest.

Exercise also makes your brain and body feel good. Just remember to protect your brain with safety gear. Wear a helmet when you ride a bicycle or do other fast activities.

Fact:

After you exercise, your body makes a chemical that helps your brain learn. Are you struggling with a math problem? Take an exercise break and try again later!

Amazing but True!

Have you ever had an ice cream headache or "brain freeze"? First, something very cold touches the roof of your mouth. Then the temperature sets off nerves that control blood flow to your head. This causes blood vessels in the head to get bigger. Your head begins to hurt. The pain isn't dangerous. You can help it by eating more slowly.

Glossary

axon (AK-sahn)—the part of a nerve cell that sends out signals

cerebellum (ser-ah-BELL-uhm)—a small part of the back of the brain that helps you balance and move

cerebrum (suhr-EE-bruhm)—the main part of the brain where thinking, feeling, and remembering take place

dendrite (DEN-drite)—a branch on a nerve cell that receives signals

hypothalamus (hye-poh-thal-uh-muhss)—your brain's temperature control

involuntary (in-VOL-uhn-tehr-ee)—done without a person's control

nerve (NURV)—a thin fiber that carries messages between the brain and other parts of the body

nucleus (NYOO-klee-uhss)—the command center of the cell that gives instructions to the other parts of the cell

spinal cord (SPY-nuhl KORD)—a thick cord of nerves that carries signals to the rest of the nerves in the body; the spinal cord carries signals both to and from the brain

Read More

Gray, **Susan H.** *The Nervous System*. The Human Body. Mankato, Minn.: Child's World, 2014.

Kolpin, Molly. *A Tour of Your Nervous System*. First Graphics: Body Systems. North Mankato, Minn.: Capstone Press, 2013.

Riley, Joelle. *Your Nervous System*. Searchlight Books: How Does Your Body Work? Minneapolis: Lerner Publications, 2013.

Internet Sites

FactHound offers a safe, fun way to find Internet sites related to this book. All of the sites on FactHound have been researched by our staff.

Here's all you do:
Visit *www.facthound.com*
Type in this code: 9781491420669

 Super-cool stuff! Check out projects, games and lots more at **www.capstonekids.com**

Critical Thinking Using the Common Core

1. How do nerves work with your brain to control your body's actions? (Key Ideas and Details)

2. What causes ice cream headaches? How can you make sure they don't happen to you? (Integration of Knowledge and Ideas)

3. Explain how reflexes protect your body. (Key Ideas and Details)

Index